The Rake
Tristram Fane Saunders

the poetry business

Published 2022 by
New Poets List
The Poetry Business
Campo House,
54 Campo Lane,
Sheffield S1 2EG

ISBN 978-1-914914-20-1
eBook ISBN 978-1-914914-21-8
Typeset by The Poetry Business
Printed by Biddles, Sheffield

The Poetry Business are a member of Inpress:
www.inpressbooks.co.uk

Distributed by IPS UK, 1 Deltic Avenue,
Rooksley, Milton Keynes MK13 8LD

The Poetry Business gratefully acknowledges
the support of Arts Council England.

Supported using public funding by
ARTS COUNCIL
ENGLAND

Malcontents

The Rake Takes His Time

(from you, reader   you'll hardly feel it, but

you'll feel it   a page

is not   a one-way mirror

that papercut   was not a papercut)

The Rake Invites You to the Weepies

Don't be lugubrious, my newest friend.
Bite lugubrious. Roll it around,
and roll around in it. Take a dive
in its lubricious, bleak lagoon, lukewarm
and wallowsome. Drink deep and swoon – the salt
will lift you like a vast and sudden futon,
a waterbed, luxurious and soft
and overfed, the kind they advertise

in why-oh-widescreen at the multiplex.
The eyeless ushers mutter   *unless*   *unless*
– shush. The trailers are my favourite bit.
It's dark in here. Can you remember where
we wandered in from? Good. Forget about it
while I brush this popcorn from your hair.

The Rake Would Like You

in a moment, but not yet, to pour
yourself out of that little peignoir
    and into the wet. The feet,
    you will notice, are clawed,
    a word which once
        meant flattered.
      It referred
to when what soothes is sharp
    – my back or yours? –
    to days when a
    soft soap approach
would scarcely scratch
the surface, but to scratch
    beneath the lather, lover,
    to scrape, to lathe,
would bring relief, brimful and hot and as
    we've time to kill, duckie,
    isn't it funny
how we find our own terms for the act 'to fill'?
      (The taps become
      a pair of snubnosed guns, a duel,
      my hand on hot and yours on cool.)
How I 'draw', partner, and you 'run'?

Laura's Song

less than I was, more than I will be
      lift me back up – you drained me, fill me
never me not, love, just until me
      left it a touch too late to kill me
lying alone so long might chill me
      dreaming we'll make amends – but will we?
            will we?

The Rake Takes a Questionnaire

Age: — No.

Occupation: — Empty.

Star sign: — O.

Blood type: — Any.

Place of birth: — The womb.

Who would you most like to meet? — It's 'whom'.

Favourite film: — Cling.

Favourite song: — I never sing,

although I dance, of course.

Do you mean...

Let's see – what's yours?

Did I say it did?

to give

in full

Status:

Married, single, divorced.

Does that matter?

Remember

your answers

sentences.

The Rake's Apology

Darling, let me lay it at your feet,
blinking and soft, a helpless little fox cub
huddled inside a gingham picnic basket
on a cold night, on your doorstep, the fog
a clean slate, no sign of the coming flurry,

the never-ending blizzard. Do not worry.
Though it may break things, let it be your dog.
Snowed in, you'll feed it steak tartare and brisket,
its licked-clean bowl the colour of false love,
of the ice outside the window, of its teeth.

The Rake's Apology (Slight Return)

I'm sorry, *but*. I'm sorry *if*. I'm sorry
that I wield apology as golfclub,
catchphrase, cordless power tool, receipt
or second-place rosette – and never biscuit,
olive branch, small origami frog.

Like Pegasus (a fine dead horse to flog)
if caught I'll wing it on the hoof. I'll busk it
improvising ifs like gold from wheat,
my spin spun bright and poisonous as foxglove.
If not, I'm not the fox you'd die to marry.

Laura's Cento

from Weldon Kees

'The keys are like old yellow teeth.'
You frequently compare yourself.

I sit in the smoky room, reading your book again,
when midnight closes in and takes away your name,
and difficult to see is where you are and where I am.

When they speak of you, they feel the need
for another day; a refuge, permanent, with trees

outside and inside. Where I go,
the present stumbles home to bed.
The ending is your own.

from The Unauthorised Biography, Vol IV: 1730–1960

He spent twelve decades polishing his craft,
studiously darkening the floorboards
in dens of moderate iniquity,

or decorating red-light district windows
with his gaunt reflection; hand-in-hand
with syphilis and debt, he whiled away

ten years in private, plain or padded cells,
then out again into the brittle evening,
pockets rich with laudanum, neglected

correspondence, old French letters, borrowed
neckerchief and snuff-box, borrowed pearls.
The latest melancholy smile perfected

daily in his little shaving-mirror.
After a lifetime of these skits and turns,
playing to the gallery each morning

and to the private boxes every night,
like a slow, malignant growth around him,
unnoticed, the world began to change.

Years pass. He lurches up the gilded stair
from *cad* to *rogue* to *fiend* to *devil*, till
tripping on *national treasure* he alights,

breathless, on the upper landing: *myth*.
And like all myths, not quite the thing it was,
elevated now to something less

than truth, he grows familiar: a click,
a whirr, the tired back-and-forward whip
of drying polaroid, and in no time

to speak of, his name dissolves: a sugar cube,
relaxing into absinthe. All politeness,
the Rake agrees to sign his photograph,

tousling the ringlets of the youngest fan,
kissing the ringless fingers of the eldest,
and all the while remembering the tale

of how the pampered fox became the dog,
and Narcissus in winter, how he watched
his own reflection as it turned to ice.

The Rake Packs Up His Troubles in an Old Kitbag and Smiles, Smiles, Smiles

Holding things, I found, was holding me
up. So nowadays I'm mostly empty-
handed, bearing nothing but the stitched
shoulder strap to this, my dashing hell-
for-leather holdall – the mark of a life spent
all over. These last few years or so, I've gathered
nothing that would make it stretch or crack.

Nothing. That's what made it stretch and crack
all over: these last few years. Or so I've gathered,
for leather holds all the marks of a life spent
with shoulders strapped to this, my dashing hell.
Hunted, baring nothing, I've been stitched
up so nowadays I'm mostly empty,
holding things I found were holding me.

The Rake's Carriage

By which I do not mean my gait.
Not my bearing, but what bore me. If it bored me,
I'd another by the time the hooves had stopped.
A *Bounder* goes on four wheels and a *Hansom* man on two,
so what was I? A sphinx of *Four-in-Hand* at morning,
two by day, and every night the *Three
Horse Shay*. I'd flit from *Whim* to *Whiskey*,
Bandy to *Berlin*. My every car a *Jaunting Car*,
I'd spin the wheels and win, the world my ostler's oyster,
a sweet amuse *Barouche*. Somewhere between
the *Calabash* and *Carryall*, I traded
Fly for *Drag*. My creditors took up the *Chaise*,
reined in the *Dos-à-Dos* and hit the *Brake*.
I saw eight-legged *Tarantasses* in my dreams
and woke inside the *Britzka 'Flying Coffin'*.
When even that was gone, I'd nothing
but this stick-thin *Spider Phaeton*
and a sidling crabwise *Jingle*
'entirely peculiar to Cork'.

These days, my friend, I'd rather walk.

The Rake Makes Lemonade

or something like it. It's an old
recipe of mine. I take
a watched pot, a naked flame,
   let them meet. Fill it
with all the crystal sugar it can hold.
   Test the water: see how little
is just enough to hide each grain, then heat
sweetness till it's hot enough to scald.
   A *simple syrup*, this is called.

With patience and the proper tools,
pare off each fingernail of zest.
In hot and sickly water, watch
   it soften as its bitter
essence, its inimitable taste
   is dissipated in the seething
pool, then set aside. Until it's cool.
At this point it is customary to cut
   the fruit – stab, twist tines through it

over a cup of colder water,
catch each drop. And when they stop,
look at what's left: squeezed out, flayed,
   poor, bare, forked.
This is a recipe for lemonade.
   When life – or too much living – *hands*
you golden worlds stretched out of shape, make syrup.
You'll need it later for that sour cup.
   The mix is all, my friend. Make plans.

Laura's Invitation

The invitation was a scribble on a folded card.
At the corner of [illegible] *and* [something] *Boulevard,*
press the bell for number [blank] *and call my name, or knock*
and call another name. The door is open, or unlocked.
How could I refuse? I could, of course, but had forgotten
how. I found the place as promised. The bannister was rotten.
I climbed the steps and waited at the golden ballroom door.
The thing was cheaply painted. Through the layered gilt, I saw
deep cracks. Through the keyhole, caught a fragment of the scene:
the ones you were were dancing with the ones I might have been.

The Rake's Looking Glass

Looking very glass indeed.
Wanting nothing, wanting need
and abstinence for once, a seed
of something weak among the weed,
he lets his thoughts lead where thoughts lead:
to Laura, and his one good deed.
Rake turns the other cheek to read
a spiderwebbed yet jangling screed
in lines that crawl his face and breed:
a bleeding heart is prone to bleed
and what's been flayed cannot be fleed
you're in her debt until she's freed
Reflecting on this backwards creed,
he turns to leave. He pays no heed.

His mirrored self kneels down to plead.

The Rake Regrets to Inform You

and you will be informed by my regret,
rewarded by it. Might we say enriched?

Not like a shrewd investor, more like water
is, to pearl our sharkies fluoride bright.

To form you, I regret. My sacrifice
is like that tooth-white bird who bibs his breast

in red to deem the young – that's you, my dear –
redeemed, reformed. Fed up with re- and in-

formation, I'll regret. Was it the egret,
or the tundra swan? So, set upon

this open bar, my barrel-chest, sate what
we might for want of better words misname

your thirst for knowledge, innocency's best
coroner. The cormorant? Oh pet.

'A sadder and a wiser' everyone
remembers that bit *'water water'* every-

one recalls *'all creatures great'* etc,
all the creatures, all except the *'Spirit'*

underneath nine fathoms' ice, unholy.
Wholly undescribed except he *'bideth*

20

by himself' and that until she died
he *'loved'* – another cheap, ill-fitting, flitting

word – that lonely bird, my Laura, Laura
knew her name. I think it rhymed with loss.

The Music Box

is like a fish eye, lidless,
undrowning underwater.
The ocean bed a witness
to the melody that caught her:

yesterday's tomorrows
have lost their someday shine
I promised I would follow
but the road we took was mine

The bow-legged ballerina
still waltzes with her sailor.
The tune grows weaker, leaner,
as she loses her regalia:

yesterday's tomorrows
have lost their someday shine
I promised I would follow
but the road we took was mine

The frail and rusted handle
isn't handled any more.
A murmur in the mantle
creaks its Mariana jaw:

yesterday's tomorrows
have lost their someday shine
I promised I would follow
but the road we took was mine

Her lover is no sailor.
Rake's dance is not a dance.
She knew that he would fail her
from that first unblinking glance:

yesterday's tomorrows
have lost their someday shine
I promised I would follow
but the road we took was mine

A pair of lifeless lovers
twirl round their lidless world.
No stars now shine above her.
His sails are all unfurled.

Laura's Letter

All-enveloping, our almost life
put the elope in envelope (along
with love and pen, the e of empty
promises, the better part of envy,
and eleven PO boxes filled
with air – my living breath, immaculately
labelled: HANDLE WITH THE UTMOST CARE).

With no return address to turn to,
only 'tomb', it may concern you
to recall our correspondence
now that all I am is post-. You talk the talk,
my less-than-love, so SWALK the SWALK .
Please find enclosed *please find me* find
enclosed your one-way fare.

the rake makes amends / a skipping song

one

the rake makes amends
from skin and loose ends
saves them for laura
the lover who lends
a silver dollar
to dance and pretend
he's not not alive

what she would call a
gentleman caller
mr rake is not
hope small   risk smaller
he's all that she's got
what could befall her
there's no second scythe

the dollar she sends
it flickers and bends
in natural light
like all the rake's friends
it doesn't look right
not something to spend
it looks like a knife

rake slips the dollar
under his collar
nicks open a vein
a thin waterfall

to fall for   he drains
his blood   rake falters
falls   opens his eyes

his attic squalor
gone   scratched fats waller
lps and chaise longue
dust and magrittes   all
the here of it gone
the landscape altered
a river of sighs

a land without land
clutched tight in his hand
the bag of amends
exactly as planned
a riverboat wends
its way up the strand
thumb out   hitch a ride

two

boatman smells trouble
rake can befuddle
prestidigitate
meddle and muddle
he tests the coin's weight
scratches his stubble
beckons rake aboard

like milk into ink
a pallid hand slinks

into his pocket
and picks   boatman blinks
an empty socket
the barge almost sinks
try not to rock it
rake's refund secured

watch rake as he goes
with sulfurtipped toes
in high cuban heels
these yellow brick roads
make souls burn   skins peel
but rake's cool as snow
the bricks are confused

whoever paved them
gouged and engraved them
with warped inventions
snares to enslave men
called   *good intentions*
rake never gave them
much notice   his shoes

skip through this unland
exactly as planned
fool bricks underfoot
with tricks underhand
the sky turns to soot
as stone turns to sand
the air is a bruise

rake's getting so close
he hears laura's ghost

not softly sleeping
coyly comatose
but cursing   weeping
all mournful-morose
she's howling the blues

three

and here's how it ends
rake lifts the amends
and tendrils of air
fill them end-to-end
from toenails to hair
merci my old friend
for my birthday suit

her voice clean as stone
like iced honeycomb
rake's tame as a tomb
and crumbles like loam
remembers the room
where he wanes alone
and looks resolute

a life for a life
that coin like a knife
slits him to pour a
small toast to his wife
laura'd adore a
drop   one would suffice
licks him like a fruit

pomegranate red
her lips where he bled
grow full as rake fades
a flick of her head
shakes warm living shades
of electric thread
stitched from tips to roots

rake wrinkles   dry   wrung
he doesn't have long
as laura escapes
the airless air throngs
with nothings all shaped
like faces rake wronged
betrayed   cheated   used

a pencilthin line
rake's lips misalign
round one last resort
the ghost of a rhyme
in a book you just bought
the rake takes his time
reader   from   you

Acknowledgements

Thank you to the editors of *Agenda, The North, New Poetries VIII, PN Review* and *The White Review*, where versions of some of these poems first appeared. Thank you to Michael Schmidt and Ali Lewis for their advice, and to everyone at Smith|Doorstop for luring the Rake out of his attic and onto the page.

This pamphlet is for Lucia Morello.